Haddon Hall

Bakewell Derbyshire

The Home of Lord Edward Manners

Designed and Photographed by Nick McCann

Written by Bryan Cleary

Technical supervision - Matthew Limbert

The author and publisher are grateful to the writers of previous guidebooks to Haddon Hall and to Professor Antony Cox for his factual contributions to the text.

Early 19th century pencil and wash drawing of Haddon by John Constable, inscribed 'August 17th'. Private Collection

Front cover: 18th century view of Haddon with Bakewell in the background, by John Smith of Derby. Private Collection

Haddon Hall came into my family through marriage over four hundred years ago, and has existed on this site since Norman times. It was unoccupied from the 18th century until my grandfather, the 9th Duke of Rutland, returned to Haddon in the early 20th century and made its careful restoration his life's work. The gardens were created by my grandmother and give much delight to thousands of visitors every year. The Hall and gardens as we see them today are a testimony to the care and dedication of my ancestors and all those who have lived and worked here over the centuries. My father, the 10th Duke, warmly welcomed visitors to Haddon and greatly valued their contribution to the upkeep of this fine old historic house.

Now it is my turn to welcome you here. I do hope you enjoy your visit, and that you find this book both informative and stimulating.

Lord Edward John Francis Manners

Nestling in the valley of the River Wye, about two miles from the Derbyshire town of Bakewell, lies Haddon Hall. Described by Pevsner as 'the English castle par excellence' it stands proudly above the river on its limestone bluff.

Haddon is a good example of a fortified manor house, although the turrets and battlements were intended as fashionable rather than functional. Haddon presents the visitor with fine examples of medieval and Tudor architecture and magnificent gardens restored in the early 20th century by the 9th Duchess of Rutland.

Once much larger, stretching almost to Sheffield and including most of Bakewell, the estate still includes the village of Alport and part of Rowsley. The village of Nether Haddon to the west of Haddon Hall fell victim to the Black Death in the 14th century and by the late 16th century had been finally abandoned.

In the middle ages much of the woodland and pasture now known as Haddon Fields would have been devoted to strip-farming, in addition to which, the income of the estate was supplemented by quarrying and lead-mining. By the end of the 13th century the Vernon family also held land in Cumbria, Cheshire, Staffordshire, Leicestershire and Buckinghamshire.

EARLY HISTORY

Questions remain as to the early history of the estate. Although the villages of Over Haddon and Nether Haddon are mentioned in Domesday Book of 1086, there is no record of a house at Haddon. However at the beginning of the 12th century the Avenel family held land at Haddon as tenants of William Peverel I. The first mention of a house and chapel, probably built around 1150, occurs in a settlement of 1180 whereby it became the property of Avice, elder daughter of William Avenel II. It remained in the Vernon family until passing to the present owners, the Manners family, in 1567.

Built of Derbyshire gritstone and limestone, the hall seems originally to have followed the plan of a Norman fort with a curtain wall enclosing a courtyard and defensive tower; the Eagle, or Peverel Tower. We know that around 1195 Richard de Vernon was granted permission by John, Count of Mortain (soon to be King John) to build an enclosing wall (below), around the tower, chapel and other, probably wooden, buildings which comprised Haddon. This wall was to be no more than 12 feet high – hardly a fortification – and was sufficient only to deter marauding outlaws. It was not until the 14th century that the walls were raised and battlements added during the re-construction of the house by Sir Richard Vernon VI which was begun in 1370. However, the larger windows of this later building phase suggest that defence was by then no longer a priority and instead emphasise the wealth and status of the owners.

St John's Wall

Banqueting Hall

Of the earliest building, little remains although examples of Norman masonry survive in parts of the Eagle Tower as well as along the south and west walls. The chapel also contains a Norman pillar and font in the south aisle and Norman lancet windows on the adjacent south wall.

In addition to the extensions to the walls, this period also saw the building of the Great Hall (above), which was to become known as the Banqueting Hall. Together with the kitchens, these would have been separate buildings set in an open quadrangle to minimize the risk of fire spreading. The Great (or Banqueting) Hall would have been the principal living area. The Solar Chamber, now the Great Chamber, also dates from this time as do the ground floor rooms below the Long Gallery.

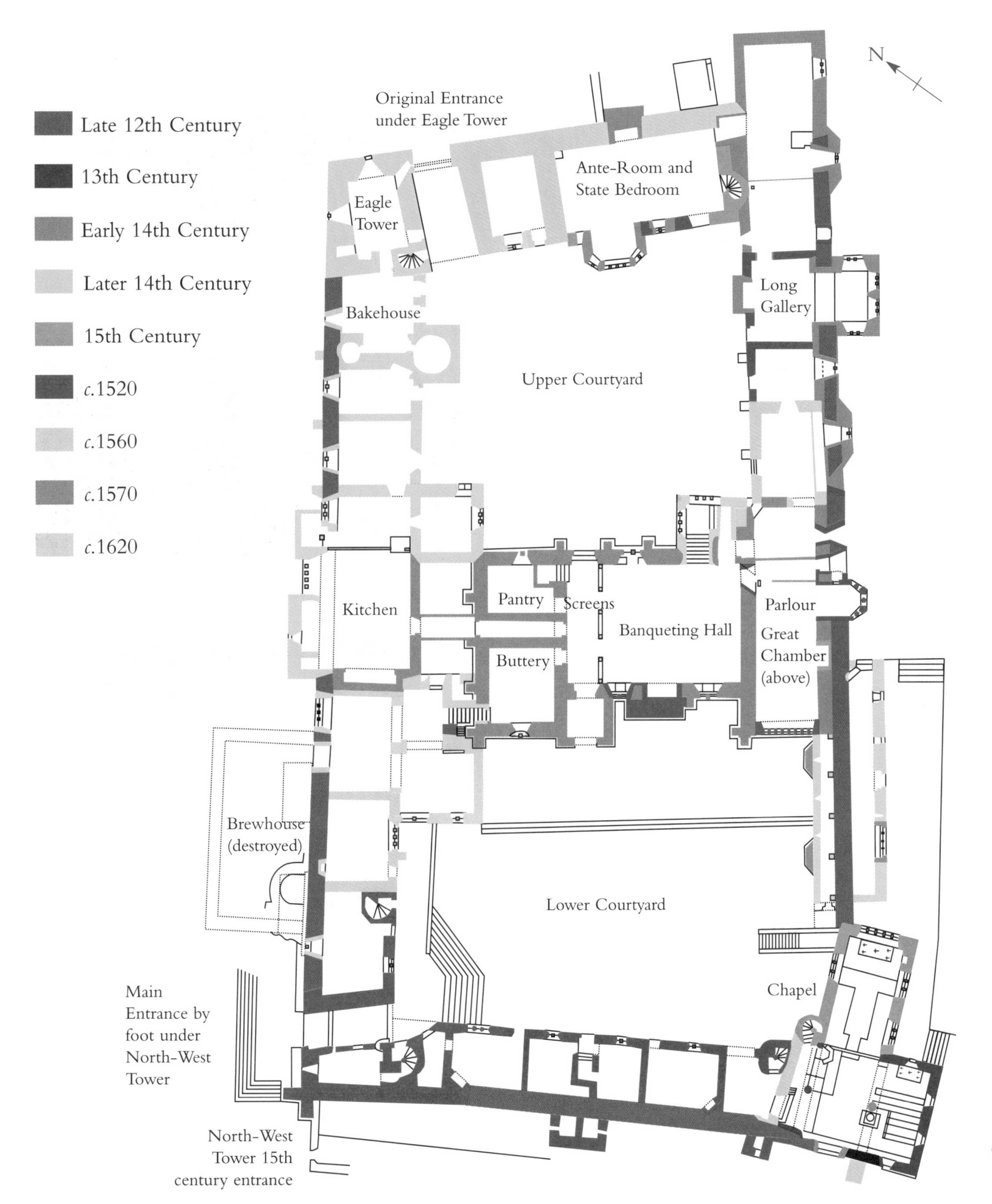
Late 12th Century
13th Century
Early 14th Century
Later 14th Century
15th Century
c.1520
c.1560
c.1570
c.1620
N
Original Entrance under Eagle Tower
Eagle Tower
Ante-Room and State Bedroom
Bakehouse
Long Gallery
Upper Courtyard
Kitchen
Pantry
Screens
Banqueting Hall
Parlour
Great Chamber (above)
Buttery
Brewhouse (destroyed)
Lower Courtyard
Chapel
Main Entrance by foot under North-West Tower
North-West Tower 15th century entrance

The Chapel was also extended, as befitted the growing importance of the manor, by the widening of the south aisle and the addition of the north aisle.

Alterations to the Chapel continued in the 15th century with the addition in 1427 of a new chancel, the Perpendicular style window above the altar and new windows in the north and south chancel walls. The second half of the 15th century saw a period of major refurbishment. Further extensions were made to the Chapel, the octagonal Bell Tower was added and the walls were decorated with fresco seccoes or 'dry' frescoes, so called to differentiate them from 'true' frescoes which are painted on the plaster while it is still wet.

In 1450 the Banqueting Hall benefited from the addition of the screen and a chimney was built on the west wall.

At the end of the century, Sir Henry Vernon created the Parlour and Great Chamber from the 14th century Solar, and commissioned the frescoes depicting the badge, of his wife Anne's family, the Talbot dog and the arms of his daughter in law Margaret's family, the Dymokes. As a spy for Thomas Cromwell, Margaret shared Anne Boleyn's bed in the Tower of London before Anne was beheaded. The decoration of this room was only completed by his grandson, Sir George Vernon.

The Norman pillar and font and the south aisle of the Chapel.

Floral design fresco seccoe.

THE 16TH CENTURY

Panelling in the Parlour or Dining Room.

Shortly before 1530, work began on building northwards, along the west wall, from the Chapel. These buildings, now the estate offices, were lodgings for guests and household officers. The North-West Tower, the present day entrance, and the buildings to the east of it towards the Kitchen were built. Other work included the lowering of the ceiling in the Kitchen and the construction of a bay window in the Parlour. Sir George Vernon later added the panelling which can be seen today.

Towards the end of the century, several rooms were altered by Sir John Manners and his wife, Dorothy Vernon, who had acquired the Hall on the death of Dorothy's father, Sir George Vernon. Their principal project was the construction of the Long Gallery in the typical Elizabethan style. The plaster ceiling shows the armorial peacock of the Manners family and the boar of the Vernons. They also re-decorated the State Bedroom.

Sir John Manners and his wife Dorothy Vernon constructed the Long Gallery

This proved to be the last phase of building. In 1703, Sir John Manners, 9th Earl of Rutland and grandson of the above, was created 1st Duke of Rutland and Marquess of Granby by Queen Anne and the family moved to Belvoir Castle, leaving Haddon Hall suspended in time. It remained uninhabited for 200 years until the 9th Duke and Duchess of Rutland in the early 20th century instituted a programme of extensive restoration which continues today.

Now, Haddon Hall is once again the family home of the Manners and it is thanks to the dedication and sympathetic touch of successive generations that it is now perhaps the foremost example in England of medieval and Tudor domestic architecture.

HADDON IN THE 19TH CENTURY: ART AND LITERATURE

It is exciting to think that Jane Austen may have written part of 'Pride & Prejudice' at Haddon, or that Sir Walter Scott used it as a setting for several of his romantic novels. These claims have been made, but sadly there is little evidence to support either. In 1846, the Baroness de Calabrella edited 'Evenings at Haddon Hall: a series of romantic tales of the olden time', illustrated with engravings by George Cattermole. Again, though some have claimed this to be a personal record of wild parties at Haddon, it appears to be a work of pure fiction. Horace Walpole, visiting in 1760, reported in a letter to George Montagu that Haddon was, 'an abandoned old castle of the Rutlands, in a romantic setting', but spoils it by adding that it 'never could have composed a tolerable dwelling'. However, in the middle of the 19th century there was interest in the Hall. For the talented Rayner family of Matlock Bath – father Samuel had exhibited at the Royal Academy before he was sixteen – it was a frequent subject. There are also two lithographs of 1872 by Joseph Nash; one of the Chapel and the other of 'the Drawing Room'.

Above all, the legend of Dorothy Vernon's elopement with John Manners fired the imagination of the Victorians. After quarrelling with Gilbert following the production of 'The Gondoliers', Sir Arthur Sullivan collaborated with Sydney Grundy in 1892 on a light opera version of the story entitled 'Haddon Hall', which ran for 204 performances. Although the libretto is mediocre it is thought by many to contain some of Sullivan's best music. Moving into the first few years of the Edwardian era, the legend crossed the Atlantic and in 1902, 'Dorothy Vernon of Haddon Hall' was published by Charles Major, a popular writer of historical romances. This was almost immediately adapted for the stage and played on Broadway, unfortunately for only 40 performances. It did, however, form the basis for the 1924 silent film of the same title starring, and possibly co-directed by, Mary Pickford. Not to be outdone, in 1903 Britain fought back with its own novella. J E Muddock, an astonishingly prolific writer, published 'Sweet "Doll" of Haddon Hall'. Both American and English versions suffer from the same faults; an unbearably pretentious style and a blithe disregard for historical truth!

ROYAL VISITORS

The earliest recorded royal visitor to Haddon was Prince Arthur, eldest brother of the future King Henry VIII, who stayed for some time in 1501 as the guest of Sir Henry Vernon, his treasurer. Despite the fact that the house was unoccupied during the 19th century, in 1872 Prince Edward (later King Edward VII), and Princess Alexandra, were entertained to a luncheon in the Great Hall at which, it is recorded, medieval dishes were served. Queen Mary, accompanied by the Duchess of Devonshire, the Duchess of Portland and Lady Mary Trefusis, came to view the progress of the 9th Duke's restoration programme in 1913. She was to return with her husband, King George V, twenty years later, 'The Times' reporting that 'the King and Queen … motored this morning to Haddon Hall and called on the Duke and Duchess of Rutland'. His signature, dated 1933, can be seen above the small fireplace in the Earl's Apartment (page 49), together with those of two members of the present Royal Family, Prince Charles and Princess Anne, dated 1979.

THE MUSEUM

As restoration of the Hall got under way in the early years of the 20th century, the 9th Duke of Rutland and his team began to find small everyday objects, lost or thrown away, evocative of the lives of the Hall's past occupants. A child's shoe (1), or the brass and beechwood washing tallies (2), used to keep a record of individual items of linen or clothing, can give us an insight into the everyday life of former times. The shilling coin from the reign of Edward VI (1547-53) found in the Chapel, represented a workman's wage for three days' thatching; the hornbook (3), inscribed with the alphabet and a prayer, tells us something about a child's education while cards and dice (4), evoke scenes of nights of gambling where fortunes could be gained, or lost!

Fortunately for us, the Duke recognised the importance of these finds and established the Museum in which to display them.

Other exhibits include a plaster reredos showing the Last Supper which is probably German in origin and dating from the 15th century. A photograph records the arrival in 1920 of a new beam for the reconstruction of the Banqueting Hall roof and in the centre of the Museum there is a rare, short-pendulum turret clock which originally stood in the Chapel belfry. The shorter of the two firearms on display is a naval boarding musket, believed to have belonged to Lord Robert Manners who was a captain in the navy.

THE ESTATE AND ITS VILLAGES OF ALPORT AND ROWSLEY

The River Wye at Rowsley

At the beginning of the 20th century, a stage coach ran between Rowsley Station and Haddon Hall; this particular one is named 'Dorothy Vernon'.

Despite its name being of Saxon origin, the present buildings of this pretty hamlet at the southern end of Lathkilldale date from the 17th and 18th centuries. The River Lathkill flows through the village over a number of weirs to join the River Bradford. Near the confluence of these, by a weir, stands an old water mill which retains its 6.5m diameter wheel. There are records of a corn mill here in 1159, which could be that mentioned in Doomsday Book as being at nearby Youlgreave. Lead was mined in the vicinity in the 18th and 19th centuries and a constant danger was that the mines would become flooded. In 1766, work began on a sough, or drain, to take floodwater four-and-a-half miles from Alport to the River Derwent at Rowsley. Completed in 1787, Hillcarr Sough was the largest in the country and had cost £32,000 but paid for itself within 2 years. In 1881, the River Bradford broke into it and disappeared from its usual course for several years until the breach was sealed up, whereupon it reappeared above ground.

Great Rowsley is situated where the A6 from Bakewell makes a sharp turn right into Darley Dale and Matlock, while Little Rowsley is found to the left on the minor road to Chatsworth. Together, they make up the village of Rowsley. There are two hotels; 'The Peacock Hotel' was built for John Stevenson, land agent to the Manners family, (the inscription bearing his name and date 1652 can still be seen above the doorway, pictured left), while 'The Grouse and Claret' formerly 'The Station', was built after 1849 when the railway arrived in the village.

The railway was closed in 1868, but in 1975 a group of enthusiasts formed the Peak Railway Society with the aim of restoring the line from Matlock to Buxton. The northern terminus is currently at Rowsley, with steam trains running on Sundays throughout the year. The parish church, dedicated to St Katherine, was built in 1855 and houses the tomb chest of Lady Catherine Manners, the second wife of the 7th Duke of Rutland.

A water mill has existed here on the River Wye for over 400 years. The present flour mill was built in 1874 by John Caudwell and was operated by the family for over 100 years. Spread over four floors the machinery, most of which predates the First World War, is driven by two water turbines and operates on most days. The building itself is Grade II listed. As well as a shop selling the mill's products there is also a café and craft centre. Across the road is Peak Village, a factory outlet shopping centre.

D'EWES COKE, ESQUIRE, 1774-1856

Land Agent from 1811 to 1856 to John 5th Duke of Rutland for his Derbyshire property, sitting in his study in the estate office, Castle Hill, Bakewell.
By OCTAVIUS OAKLEY, 1800-1867 Signed and dated 1831.

Behind the Land Agent are pictures of the Estate's properties (top row): The Fox Inn, Longshaw; Castle Hill, Bakewell; and Longshaw Lodge, Sheffield. (Bottom row): Stanton Woodhouse, Rowsley; Haddon Hall; and The Peacock Inn, Rowsley

THE TAPESTRIES

The tapestries on display in the Hall are all that remain of a much larger collection, the rest having been destroyed by fire in 1925. Having remained hanging throughout the 200 years in which the Hall was unoccupied, the 9th Duke had them removed to a room in the stable block for safety during his restoration work. The irony of this is recorded by the Duke himself in his notebook; 'at about 11.15 pm on the night of June 1st 1925 a disastrous fire broke out in the tea-room over the stables at Haddon...the majority of the Haddon tapestry was stored in a room at the north end of the building, the consequence being that all the tapestries in this room were burnt or partially so'. Approximately 60 pieces were destroyed or damaged beyond repair. Those which could be were restored and re-hung in the Hall. The most important tapestries are those depicting the five senses made in Mortlake in the early 17th century. It is believed that these fine examples of English tapestry work may have belonged to Charles I. Following his execution in 1649, the Council of State ordered that the Royal tapestries be sold and the inventory of sale records that lot 150 (Senses Tapestries) was sold for £270. On the right hand corner, the monogram 'PDM' is that of Philip de Maecht, a master weaver known to have been working between 1620 and 1623. The other monogram, 'CF', is that of Sir Francis Crane who was in charge of the Mortlake factory from 1619 until his death in 1636.

All five tapestries have survived. 'Seeing' hangs above the Minstrels' Gallery in the Great Hall. On the landing are 'Hearing', 'Tasting', and 'Feeling', while the last of the series, 'Smelling', hangs in the Ante-room of the State Bedroom.

The State Bedroom houses a fine set of very colourful Brussels tapestries showing hunting scenes dating from the first half of the 16th century (opposite). Note the humorous detail in the one to the left of the fireplace in which a horse is apparently deliberately treading on the foot of a pikeman.

Detail of a tapestry hanging to the left of the fireplace in the Earl's Apartment.

Photograph: © Skyscan/ W. Cross

Tour of the House

The approach to the Hall has changed little in 300 years. The walk by the beech hedge from the Gatehouse with its massive oak-studded doors affords glimpses of the Hall through the trees before you emerge into the open. To the left you can see a dovecote dating from the 16th century.

Details from the **Rex Whistler painting** of Haddon in the Long Gallery, showing the 16th century Dovecote and the bridge over the River Wye, (and below), topiary in the private garden next to the Restaurant.

Crossing the bridge over the River Wye brings us first to the Elizabethan stables. During the restoration of the Hall in the early years of the 20th century, the 9th Duke of Rutland installed modern kitchens, linked to the Tudor kitchen by a 47 yard tunnel. These kitchens now serve the present-day licensed restaurant which is on the upper floor and has extensive views over the Wye valley and surrounding countryside. In the cottage garden to the left, the topiary yew trees have been created into the shapes of a peacock and a boar's head which are, respectively, the arms of the Manners and Vernon families.

Here, the driveway turns before beginning the ascent to the main entrance in the North-West Tower, to the right of which is a short flight of stone steps, in the past used as a mounting block. The steps to the left led to the now demolished brew house.

The **North-West Tower** became the entrance to the Hall in the early 16th century. The building was begun by Sir Henry Vernon in the last years of the 15th century and completed in the 1530s by his grandson, Sir George Vernon. The Vernon coat of arms can be seen above the window of the Tower (above).

THE NORTH-WEST TOWER AND LOWER COURTYARD

On passing through the entrance we find ourselves in the Lower Courtyard. From here you can appreciate the way in which the Hall has evolved. The mixture of building styles from the different periods of its history is given coherence by the use of grey limestone and yellow gritstone, although buildings have been added at different times with, apparently, little planning.

To our right are the Tudor buildings added by Sir Henry Vernon. These were to house the household and estate officials, and remain the administrative offices of the estate. Looking back at the gateway through which you entered you will notice the ingenious way in which it has been incorporated by the use of a complex series of squinches. In order to link the office wing with the earlier tower without blocking up the gateway, you will see how the house has been 'bent'. This retains structural security and is also an aesthetically pleasing solution.

We can also see in the right hand corner the Chapel, the octagonal bell tower erected by Sir William Vernon and, adjacent to it, the earlier 15th century wing now known as the Earl's Apartments.

On the left side of the courtyard the Kitchen and Banqueting Hall form the heart of the medieval house. The porch, chimney and battlements were added about 1430: notice the skilfully carved gargoyles on the porch extension to the left of the Banqueting Hall and the coats of arms of the Vernon and Manners families, the boar's head and peacock respectively, on the lead pipes. These mark the progress of the building and a few have both crests, showing that they must have been put up after John Manners and his wife Dorothy Vernon inherited the Hall in 1567.

The Courtyard seen from the entrance to the Chapel.

Opposite: Three early archive photographs of the Courtyard, the lower one showing the octagonal bell tower and to the right, the entrance to the Chapel

King John's Wall

In 1193, Richard de Vernon was granted a licence by John, Count of Mortain, to build a wall of not more than twelve feet in height enclosing the Chapel, the Watch Tower and a number of timber buildings. Prince John was to become king four years later on the death of his brother, Richard I.

Known as King John's Wall it was, over the years, to be incorporated into the fabric of the Hall as it was extended and the section you see here is all that remains visible. In the 15th century an open walkway was created and you can see from the revealed area the simple but effective means by which this was achieved using five massive cantilever oak posts. Fashions change, however, and 100 years later the walkway was enclosed creating a long narrow room with the Earl's Apartments above.

THE CHAPEL

Dedicated to St Nicholas and originally the parish church of Nether Haddon, the Chapel was extended over the years and contains examples of some of the earliest masonry in the fabric of the Hall.

On entering you see before you the Norman pillar and arches dividing the north and south aisles which make up the nave. The south aisle dates from the mid 12th century and was widened during the 15th century when the north aisle was added. The date (1427) and the initials of Sir Richard Vernon and his wife which appear in the east window above the altar are evidence that the chancel was built at this time. One of the roof beams is inscribed 'G.M. 1624' which suggests that the roof was repaired or replaced in that year by Sir George Manners. The faces of the saints portrayed in the stained glass were, unfortunately, stolen in 1828 and even a reward of one hundred guineas failed to recover them. A flight of oak stairs leads to the music gallery. The Chapel is still the parish church of Nether Haddon which is one of the smallest parishes in the country.

Box Pews

These high-sided oak pews probably date from the 16th century and were for the family and their guests. They are separated from the pews behind by an elaborately wrought Gothic screen and have a panelled front incorporating fragments of the Rood Screen, the upper section of which is railed. The four doors retain their original wrought-iron hinges.

Font

The circular Norman stone font, late 11th to late 12th century, is lead lined with an iron staple. The oak cover with its turned bulbous centre pillar supporting four double-curved scroll-bracket arms is Jacobean.

Effigy of Lord Haddon

The marble effigy is of Robert Charles John Manners, Lord Haddon, the son of the 8th Duke of Rutland. As the eldest son he would have inherited the Hall but died at the age of 9 in 1894. As a final tribute to him, his grief-stricken mother, Violet, sculpted the effigy of him which now lies in the chapel at Belvoir Castle. This copy, in Italian marble, was made for the chapel at Haddon.

The Rood Screen

In the upper part of the north wall (the left as you face the altar) you can see a small door. In the corresponding position on the south wall, next to the Norman arches, there is a squint or hagioscope, which is an oblique slit giving a view of the altar. Between these, the Rood Screen, separating the chancel from the nave, once stood. There would have been a gallery on top to which the door in the north wall would have given access.

Pews (south aisle) and Pulpit (north aisle)

There are five pews in the south aisle which would have been for the Hall servants. Made of oak, with sturdy stretchers, they can be dated to 1632 on evidence from the steward's account book for that year which records:

Pd Robt. Taylor his bill for Cutting and squareing timber and making seats in the chappell - £2 17s. 8d.

Pd Matthew Bagshawe for 4 daies worke for the ground worke of the pulpit & making the long seate - £0 04s. 0d.

Entrance to the Pulpit which is six-sided and panelled, with a carved frieze, is by means of a door. Some of the moulding has been gilded.

The Fresco Seccoes

These paintings were originally brightly coloured, a suggestion of which remains high above the main door and on the wall above the arches. Also on this wall is an image of St Christopher, the patron saint of travellers. In the south aisle you will see three skeletons portrayed: these are fragments of a much larger painting which would have included three kings and would have illustrated a medieval Morality of earthly vanity. In the chancel there are illustrations of the lives of St Nicholas and St Anne and the south wall is covered in an attractive leaf design. St Nicholas was from early times associated with the Chapel. The marriage settlement of 1180 made between William Avenel and his sons in law, Simon Bassett and Richard Vernon, refers to 'the chapel of St Nicholas' and the will of Sir Henry c.1514 mentions 'That there be a priest perpetual singing and there abiding in the chapel in Neder Haddon according to the will of my grandfather, there to serve God, Saint Nicholas and Saint Anne and to pray for my soul, my grandfather's soul, my wife's soul and for all the souls that come of my grandfather'.

It is thought that these fresco seccoes were commissioned by Richard Vernon VI in the early 15th century when other modifications to the Chapel were made. The fate of these fine examples of early church decoration is typical of that which befell similar work in churches throughout the country during the Reformation. They were plastered over and the walls whitewashed: there is evidence of deliberate defacement. We know that traces of these frescoes could be seen in the 19th century, but it was the 9th Duke of Rutland who, during his restoration work on the Hall in the early 20th century, caused them to be fully uncovered and carefully restored by Professor E W Tristram, a leading authority on ecclesiastical painting. The work of conservation and restoration continues today.

Detail of the 'three skeletons'

Detail of St Christopher carrying Christ

St Nicholas calming the storm

and resurrecting three children

15th century stained glass

The windows contain some fine 15th-century painted glass. Sadly in the early 19th century, during the house's desertion, much of the glass was stolen. A reward of one hundred guineas at the time failed to recover the glass. What we see today is a rearrangement of the remaining original glass.

The Reredos

The Nottingham alabaster reredos dates from the 15th century and was bought in 1933 by the 9th Duke. Originally containing 11 panels portraying scenes of the Passion, these are now reduced to 9. The wooden frame was made in 1933 and the gilded Latin inscriptions were copied from a 15th century frame in the National Museum of Iceland in Reykjavik. As part of his programme of restoration the 9th Duke himself fitted the panels into the frame. It is thought that the oak carving which crests the reredos was once part of the Rood Screen. The canvas altar frontal depicting the Manners and Vernon arms was also painted in 1933.

Leaving the Chapel, we now cross the Courtyard to the porch of the Banqueting Hall. To our left in the porch is a Roman altar dedicated to Mars found in the fields of the estate. From the Screen Passage we turn left into the Kitchen.

The Bakery

The Bakery contains a 17th century kneading trough and two domed bread ovens. There also remains the base of an electric serving lift to the Nursery which was installed by the 9th Duke in the early 20th century.

THE KITCHEN

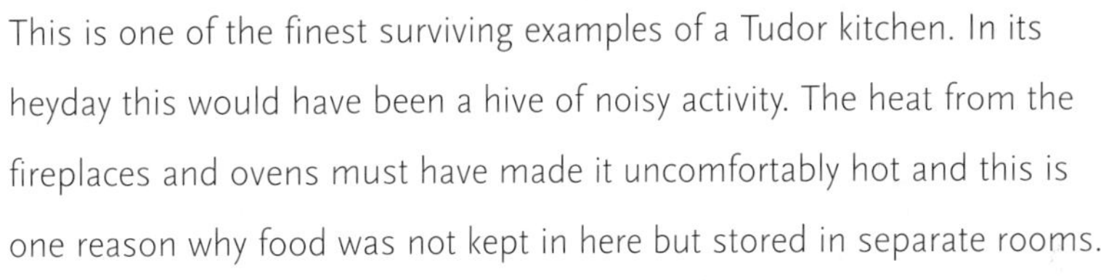

This is one of the finest surviving examples of a Tudor kitchen. In its heyday this would have been a hive of noisy activity. The heat from the fireplaces and ovens must have made it uncomfortably hot and this is one reason why food was not kept in here but stored in separate rooms.

Built in the 14th century, the Kitchen comprises a purely utilitarian set of rooms which originally stood apart from the other buildings to minimise the risk of fire spreading to the main house. The passageway linking the Kitchen to the Hall is thus a much later addition.

The main room contains a water boiler heated by a fire. On the same wall to the right is a stone trough fed by the only water system to the Hall and divided into three to hold water of varying degrees of cleanliness. Scorch marks on the timber partition wall show where candles were placed for illumination.

The fireplace flue

Next to the great fireplace stands an early 17th century log box (above left), with a sloping top, panelled sides and a linen-fold panelled front. In front of it is an oak block of the same period, probably used as a chopping block on which to split logs to feed the fire. The 16th century oak carving table which is fixed to the wall and supported by sturdy legs and stretchers shows evidence through wear to its surface of many years of food preparation.

Milk Larder

Also in the original Milk Larder are Hutches or meal arks. These were used for the storage of grain or bread. One dates from the late 15th to early 16th century and, like the other two 17th century corn bins, is simply constructed with the side and front boards fixed together with wooden pegs. Three boards are used to make the domed lid which is held in place by means of a pin hinge.

The oak side table or buffet (c.1480) originated in the west country. The ends each have a linen-fold panel. Once extendable, the extensions, and the door, are now lost and the cross stretchers bracing the legs are a later replacement.

The 'dole' cupboards

The original Milk Larder now houses probably the finest collection of 'dole' cupboards in the world. These were put outside houses such as Haddon for passing traders or Estate workers, and filled with food and leftovers from the kitchen. Made in the Gothic style, this collection is very rare as these wooden cupboards were left outside and exposed to the elements. Some are originally from Haddon and others bought by the 9th Duke. The modern phrase 'on the dole' (receiving assistance), stems from the purpose of the 'dole' cupboard.

This dole cupboard (c.1450) is made of English oak and would possibly have stood outside the Hall.

The Butchery

Before the days of canned food and refrigeration, food would be preserved here by drying, salting or pickling. The 15th century salting trough, which has always stood in this room, is formed from a single, hollowed-out, oak trunk. In large households a servant, known as 'the powderer', would crush the salt which was used to cover the meat in the process of preservation. In cooking, creamy sauces, fruit and spices were used to counteract the saltiness of the food.

The two 17th century oak hanging racks were fixed to the wall and beams and used for hanging animal carcases. It is on record that during the 17th century there were killed and eaten annually between 30 and 40 'beeves', between 400 and 500 sheep and 8 to 10 swine.

The oak block, probably 15th century like the salting trough, stands on three short legs and was doubtless used for jointing meat in preparation for salting or for catching drips from hanging meat.

The Banqueting Hall

This would have been the communal living space when it was built in the 14th century. Both family and servants would have eaten and slept here. By the beginning of the 15th century however, the family would have begun to eat in the privacy of the Great Chamber and spend their leisure time in the Parlour which acquired the function of a private sitting room. Consequently the Great Hall became a room in which to entertain and hold social events and its name was changed to the Banqueting Hall.

As in other great houses of the period the walls are panelled, which, as well as underlining the status of the family, fulfilled the more prosaic function of insulating the room to retain the heat. The chimney, added in the mid 15th century, replaced a central hearth, the original roof having vents to draw out the smoke. The Banqueting Hall was re-roofed using timbers from the Haddon and Belvoir estates in the years 1924-5 as part of the 9th Duke's restoration programme and the date 1924 is carved on one of the main beams. The screen through which you entered is a fine example of Gothic tracery and dates from about 1400. The Minstrels' Gallery above it was also constructed in the 15th century. The tapestry which hangs above the Minstrels' Gallery is one of five English tapestries produced at Mortlake in the early 17th century depicting 'The Five Senses'. The antlers around the walls date from the middle of the 17th century.

The High Table and Bench

The long table (c.1400) consists of a top made of two elm planks resting on three square pillars with splayed feet. The top is not attached to the base which allowed it to be turned over so that both sides could be used. The bench is contemporary with the table and is made of one plank on square legs, one of which has been renewed. In 1921, during the 9th Duke's restoration, both these items of furniture were treated with size to deter woodworm. The raised platform or dais on which the table stands marked the status of the Lord, his family and guests, separating them from the servants and guests of lower rank.

Behind the refectory table hangs a fine example of **French tapestry** showing the Royal Arms of England and reputedly presented to the Vernon family by King Henry VIII. Prince Arthur, Henry's eldest brother, is believed to have spent considerable time at Haddon as Sir Henry Vernon had been appointed his Governor and Comptroller and Treasurer of his household. The style of the tapestry suggests that it was made during the reign of King Edward IV (1461-1483).

The Carving Table

The 16th century oblong carving table has a heavy ash top standing on four oak legs. The deep groove cut into the top was to collect the juices from the meat.

Chest with three locks

Behind the screen is a 14th century iron-bound oak chest which came originally from St Modwen's Church in Burton on Trent where it was probably used to store parish records. It was bought in 1912 for £5 by the 9th Duke from the owner of the Rutland Arms.

Dog Gates

At the bottom of the staircase are the original 17th century dog gates. Fitted with oak pulleys and lead weights they have panelled lower portions surmounted by turned rails.

Attached to the screen you can see an iron manacle and lock. Supposedly, if a guest 'did not drink fayre' - that is, too little or too much, his punishment was to have his wrist secured in the manacle while the remainder of his drink was poured down his sleeve!

If a guest '**did not drink fayre**' his arm would be held in the manacle and the rest of his drink would be poured down his sleeve. This might not seem a great punishment, but with the infrequency of washing in those days, it was a great deterrent.

Opposite: The **painting above the fireplace** is attributed to the 17th century Dutch artist, Hondecoeter.

In the east corner of the Banqueting Hall are steps to the upper floor, and the entrance to the **Dining Room or Parlour**

The Parlour, or Dining Room

In the window recess are **carved figures in the oak panelling**. These two below are thought to be possibly Queen Elizabeth of York, and her husband, King Henry VII.

In contrast to the high ceiling of the Banqueting Hall which you have just left, this typically Tudor room is cosy and intimate. The Parlour served as private quarters for the family, away from the bustle of everyday life in the Banqueting Hall, and is still used as a dining room. The dining table, commissioned by the 9th Duke of Rutland, is a copy of the High Table in the Banqueting Hall.

The plaster ceiling was installed by Sir Henry Vernon in the early 1500s and is decorated with a painted Tudor rose and Talbot dog in recognition of his marriage to Anne Talbot, the daughter of the Earl of Shrewsbury. There is also the boar's head of the Vernons and the sword and lions of the Dymoke family; Sir Henry's daughter in law being the daughter of Sir Robert Dymoke.

This room was completed in 1545 by Sir George Vernon whose initials (G.V) and those of his wife (M.V), together with the date, can be seen on the top left of the fireplace. Carved directly over the fireplace is the text based on Wycliffe's translation of the Bible (c.1395): 'Drede God and Honour the Kyng' (1 Peter 2 v.17). Above this are carvings of the Royal Tudor Arms and the Prince of Wales' feathers with the initials 'E.P' representing the future Edward VI. In the window recess are three carved figures, possibly of King Henry VII and his Queen, Elizabeth of York, and of Will Somers, his court jester. The remainder of the frieze shows armorial shields of the Vernons and families with whom they have intermarried over the previous 300 years.

We must now return to the Banqueting Hall in order to ascend to the first floor.

The tapestries hanging in the Great Chamber were thought to be Flemish, but detail in the treatment of the foliage suggests that they are more likely to have been woven in Paris sometime before 1650.

THE GREAT CHAMBER

This room was re-roofed and given its present basic form about 1500 by Sir Henry Vernon at the same time that the Parlour was remodelled below, although the plaster ceiling in the oriel window bay and the frieze around the room are finely executed examples of early 17th century English Renaissance decoration. Within the oriel bay is a 14th century pew end with a satirical carving depicting the rapacity of the clergy. The blocked doorway probably led originally to the curtain wall walk. Traces of gold and green paint are still visible on parts of the 17th century oak panelling indicating that it was once lavishly decorated. To the left of the door on entering the chamber is a full-length charcoal and watercolour of Kathleen, 9th Duchess of Rutland, by Dame Laura Knight. This was a working sketch for the oil painting which hangs in the Picture Gallery at Belvoir Castle. Other items of interest in this room include an oak Charles II chair, a 17th century pearwood armchair with cane panelled back and a set of high-back 17th century chairs in oak. The long table, also of oak, is contemporary with these.

The 17th century tapestries, which have always hung in this room, are either Flemish or French, and are described on page 16.

Part of the 14th century house, this would originally have been **the Solar** which would have been the private quarters of the Lord and his family. Medieval manor houses often had such an upstairs room which was well provided with windows to make the most of natural light, hence the name. Many such solars are built above areas used for storage.

Before entering the Earl's Bedroom, we must first pass through a **small ante-chamber** which once served as a dressing room. Today it houses a collection of furniture and some interesting paintings. The portrait of the 6th Earl of Rutland (here), is by an unknown artist.

The full-length portrait is of Martin Middleton, a long-serving employee of the Manners family, and is said to be life-size.

A watercolour of Belvoir Castle hangs in the room, signifying the family's move there in 1703.

THE EARL'S APARTMENT

Although this room was used as a bedroom by the Earls of Rutland from 1641 until the family moved to Belvoir Castle in 1703, it may previously have had other functions. Originally two chambers, there was a small room at the far end which explains why there are two fireplaces in what is a relatively small space and the stairs leading to the Chapel below suggest a possible ecclesiastical use. During his restoration work in the early 1500s Sir Henry Vernon rebuilt this room as a Gallery and removed the partition wall: with the construction of the Long Gallery towards the end of the century this use was superseded. The room retains its original roof which initally may have been covered in plaster. Above the smaller fireplace are signatures in the plaster of visiting members of the Royal Family; King George V in 1933 and Prince Charles and Princess Anne in 1979.

George R.I. 1933

Charles 1979 Anne 1979

Items of interest include a Charles II tortoiseshell looking glass which the 9th Duke personally restored. There are also an English early 17th century spinning chair with triangular shaped seat and back and a pair of locally made chairs dating from c.1640. Two oak chests, one with Gothic roundels and dating from c.1200 and the other with a divided lid and two locks, together with a cupboard c.1500, are also to be found.

At the far end of the room, a linen-fold door (left), would have provided access to the Lower Courtyard, and thence to the Chapel, by means of an outside staircase.

If you now return to the Great Chamber and cross the landing you can ascend the semicircular steps to the Long Gallery. These steps are said to have been cut from the roots of a single oak and lead to arguably Haddon's most spectacular room.

The Long Gallery

As you enter the Long Gallery, the predominant feeling is of light and space. The many windows, south facing to make the most of the sunlight, give on to a typical Elizabethan long gallery 110 feet long and 17 feet wide.

The room was begun by Sir George Vernon and it was from here, legend has it, that his daughter Dorothy eloped, but it is thanks to Dorothy and her husband, John Manners, that we see the room as it is today.

The Long Gallery would have been used as an indoor promenade, enabling the family and their guests to take exercise by walking without chancing the vagaries of the Derbyshire climate. Its position on the upper floor of the house also afforded fine views of the gardens and surrounding countryside. Long galleries were also used for less strenuous recreation such as gaming and, in the case of the ladies, needlecraft as well as for social events such as balls.

Elsewhere the panel painting incorporates part of an earlier work portraying classical scenes and includes two figures representing the 9th Duke (with the gun) and his son, the future 10th Duke.

If you look carefully at the windows you will see that the **diamond-shaped panes** are set at different angles: as well as being visually attractive this maximises the use of the daylight. All the windows face the panelled walls which date to Sir John's modifications to the room at the end of the 16th century.

This painting of **Haddon Hall** which you see over the fireplace was commissioned by the 9th Duke of Rutland and painted by **Rex Whistler** in 1933 to commemorate the restoration of the Hall.

The set of ten late 17th century walnut chairs are intricately carved in the style of Daniel Marot and were brought from the 17th century Belvoir Castle demolished in 1800.

The panelling is predominantly of oak and was probably originally lime-washed to size the timber before being painted with designs in a foxy-red colour. It consists of classical pilasters with painted inlays and is much finer and more elaborate than in the older rooms in the house. The upper panelling consists of a frieze showing the boar's head of the Vernon family united with the peacock of the Manners interspersed with rose and thistle, a popular decorative motif of the time.

The furniture in the Long Gallery is representative of several periods. The oak dowry or vestment chest of 15th century manufacture which stands at the far end of the gallery has a carved front showing the arms of the Vernons and related families. Originally in the Chapel it is possible that this chest was used to store the title deeds of the estate.

The four oblong stools, covered in green fabric, are 17th century. The musical instrument, although often mistakenly taken to be a harpsichord, is in fact a spinet made by Thomas Hitchcock of London in the 18th century. The number 1289 is the maker's number.

We leave the Long Gallery through a **carved door surmounted by the Manners family crest**. The strange arrangement of the hinges is a self-closing mechanism, probably dating from the 9th Duke's restoration work in the 1920s.

Ante-room and State Bedroom

The State Bedroom was redecorated by Sir John Manners and Dorothy Vernon in the late 16th century. In the Ante-room we see the final tapestry, 'Smelling', of the five Senses Tapestries, and an interesting cabinet decorated with painted panels and somewhat enigmatic carvings of a man and a woman! There are other fine tapestries from Brussels in the State Bedroom, which date from the middle of the 16th century. Note the humorous detail in the one to the left of the fireplace in which a horse is apparently deliberately treading on the foot of a pikeman.

Visitors may well be puzzled by the lack of a bed. During the restoration of the Hall, the state bed of Haddon was removed to Belvoir Castle where it is kept in the Picture Gallery.

From the Ante-room a flight of worn steps leads to the gardens (right). These are known as Dorothy Vernon's steps down which she is said to have fled but the present ones date from 1649, long after her supposed elopement with John Manners. We know that in 1649 men were paid to transport the stone from Stanton Moor and for ten days' work to construct the steps. There is no record of an earlier staircase.

The plaster relief above the fireplace shows **Orpheus taming the animals**. There is no attempt at realism in the relative sizes of the various beasts and the peacock of the Manners family takes pride of place. Probably dating from the mid 1500s when elephants and monkeys would have been known only to the few, there is an artless simplicity in the depiction of these. Similar designs occur at Hardwick Hall and it is possible that these influenced the modellers of this piece at Haddon.

Some of the **window panels** in this room have been engraved by the workmen fitting them, either with poems or lists of the men's names.

THE GARDENS

When John Manners and Dorothy Vernon built the Long Gallery at the end of the sixteenth century, they also laid out the garden below its windows. Not much is known about this early planting scheme and layouts, but viewed from above, the garden would have probably been divided into square 'plots' each of which would have featured an elaborate Elizabethan knot garden with gravel paths in between. Traditionally these would have been planted with low growing herbs such as evergreen hyssop or germander, which could be sharply clipped into low hedges to form geometrical green ribbons and interweaving patterns. Together with fragrant thyme, lavender and lemon balm these knots provided not only beauty but also plants for medical purposes and food.

Entries in the Haddon account books to a 'Mr Smithstone' and to Lady Willoughby in 1582 suggests that the famous Elizabethan architect Robert Smythson – who designed the Willoughby's house and garden Wollaton Hall – was also responsible for the original garden and the Long Gallery at Haddon. Like Wollaton Hall, the garden at Haddon featured stone balustrades and steps, as well as a large terrace (which now contains a 20th century fountain and pool) that was linked to the house.

The main structure of the garden as it is today with its descending terraces was laid out in the middle of the seventeenth century, when the two top terraces (the topmost one is today closed to the public) and the lower garden (also closed to the public) were created. This was a typical arrangement for a late Renaissance garden in England which had been originally inspired by the gardens of Italian hill-top villas.

The yews on the upper terrace were cut down and younger yew trees planted; the ivy was stripped from the walls and balustrades and replaced with **climbing roses**, many of which remain today, and the herbaceous border was created at the foot of the top retaining wall.

At the same time the Duchess had the pond and fountain installed on what is now known as the **Fountain Terrace**. This served the dual purpose of attractive water feature and paddling pool for the children. Over the years the gardens have grown and matured but it is thanks to the 9th Duke and Duchess that we can enjoy them in their present magnificence.

Built for pleasure and show, many of these Renaissance gardens featured cascading waterworks, fountains and parterres laid out in elaborate patterns.

While other formal gardens received a 'landscape' make-over in the eighteenth century by gardeners such as Lancelot Brown, who razed elaborate parterres, softened geometrical terraces and pulled down balustrades, Haddon survived unscathed because the Manners family preferred to live in the more fashionable Belvoir Castle – mostly ignoring Haddon. Though the planting grew wild, topiary became unruly and ivy gained the upper-hand, the basic structure of the garden remained untouched by the fashions of the time. So Haddon continues to be a fine example of an English Renaissance garden.

The garden the visitor sees today exists thanks to the careful and thorough restoration by the 9th Duke and his wife when they returned to Haddon Hall at the beginning of the 20th century. They stripped the overgrown walls and balustrades of ivy, and planted roses and clematis instead. They also added the herbaceous borders and felled the overgrown trees, as well as building the pool on the Fountain Terrace and restoring the stonework.

Today an abundance of clematis and roses throw the old walls of Haddon into an kaleidoscope of colour, competing with the thirty to forty varieties of delphiniums which range from whites and yellows through to pinks and dark blues. And standing amidst this blaze of colour, the visitor can see the river Wye weaving its course through the meadows. Across it, is Dorothy Vernon's Bridge, a little stone bridge of which legend says it was the very place where John Manners waited to elope with Dorothy one night in the late sixteenth century.

Dorothy Vernon's Bridge crossing the River Wye.

In the **Wye valley** the limestone of the White Peak meets the gritstone of the Dark Peak. The soil is loose and poor and requires a great deal of mulching to improve its structure and water retention. The situation is complicated by the garden's terraces which encourage rapid drainage.

In time for the arrival of the first visitors towards the end of March, the narcissi and tulips which were planted in autumn will be in full flower, together with the aubrietia and cherry blossom. These are succeeded in turn by the early climbing roses and clematis. Below the windows of the Long Gallery on the south side of the Fountain Terrace, copious watering and a constant battle against the slugs from April to mid-June nurture the growing delphiniums. From mid-June onwards up to forty varieties ranging through whites and yellows to pink and dark blue provide a profusion of lightly fragrant colour.

Lord and Lady
Edward Manners

THE OWNERS OF HADDON HALL

'Avenell of Haddon' (living 1103-1114)

William Avenell I (living 1114-1150) — Avice

William Avenell II (d.1194) — Hawise Waard

Sir Richard de Vernon I (d.c.1215) — Avice Avenell, daughter and coheir of William Avenell

Sir William de Vernon I (c.1181-c.1242) — Margaret, daughter and heiress of Sir Robert de Stockport

Sir Richard de Vernon II (died without issue before 1270) — Helewise, daughter of Sir Richard de Gemon

Robert de Vernon — Hawise de Brailsford

Sir Gilbert le Franceys — **Hawise de Vernon**

Sir Richard le Franceys / de Vernon III (1262-c.1329) — Isabel, daughter of Sir Michael de Harcla

Sir Richard de Vernon IV (d.1323) — Matilda, daughter and coheiress of William de Camville

Sir William de Vernon II (b.1313-before 1339) — Joan

Sir Richard de Vernon V (d.1376) — Juliana, sister and heiress of Sir Fulk de Pembrugge of Tong Castle

Sir Richard de Vernon VI (1367-1400) — Johanna, daughter of Sir Rhys ap Griffith and heiress of Roger de Stackpole

Sir Richard de Vernon VII (1390-1451) — Benedicta, daughter of Sir John de Ludlow of Hodnet

Sir William Vernon III (1418-1467) — Margaret, daughter of William Swynfen and heiress of Sir Robert Pype

Sir Henry Vernon (1441-1515) — Lady Ann Talbot, daughter of 2nd Earl Shrewsbury

Sir Richard de Vernon VIII (c.1485-1517) — Margaret, daughter, Sir Robert Dymoke

Sir George Vernon (1514/5-1565) — Margaret, daughter, Sir George Tallboys

Sir John Manners 2nd son of 1st Earl of Rutland (d.1611) — **Dorothy Vernon** (d.1584)

Sir George Manners (d.1623) — Grace, daughter, Sir Henry Pierpoint

John Manners 8th Earl of Rutland (d.1679) — Frances, daughter of Lord Montagu

John, 9th Earl of Rutland cr. Duke of Rutland & Marquis of Granby — Catherine, daughter of Viscount Campden

John, 2nd Duke of Rutland (d.1721) — Catherine, daughter of Lord William Russell

John, 3rd Duke (d.1779) — Bridget, daughter of Lord Lexington

John, Marquis of Granby (d.1770) — Frances, daughter of the Duke of Somerset

Charles, 4th Duke (d.1787) — Mary Isabella, daughter of the Duke of Beaufort

John Henry, 5th Duke (d.1857) — Elizabeth, daughter of the Earl of Carlisle

Charles, 6th Duke (d.1888)

John, 7th Duke (d.1906) — Catherine, daughter of Col. George Marlay

Henry John, 8th Duke (d.1925) — Violet, daughter of Col. Honourable C H Lindsay

Robert Charles John, Lord Haddon (d.1894)

John Henry, 9th Duke (d.1925) — Kathleen, daughter of Francis John Tennant

Charles John Henry, 10th Duke (d.1999) — Frances, daughter of Charles Francis Sweeney

David Charles Robert, 11th Duke

Lord Edward John Francis Manners

THE OWNERS OF HADDON HALL

The first recorded owners of a house on the site of Haddon Hall are the Avenel family who also held land in Buckinghamshire and Northamptonshire. The marriage settlement of 1180 made between William Avenel II and his sons in law, Richard de Vernon and Simon Bassett refers to both a house and a chapel. It was Richard de Vernon's marriage to Avice Avenel, William's eldest daughter, which brought the Vernon family to Haddon.

THE VERNONS

Most of the construction of the Hall as we see it today took place during the ownership of the Vernons between 1180 and 1565. In 1193 Richard de Vernon I was granted a licence to enclose the Chapel and other buildings within a wall 'without crenellations'. Richard de Vernon I became Sheriff of Lancashire, his son William I justice of Chester and his grandson Richard II serjeant of the king's body and castellan of Peak Castle. By the 15th century the family had become one of the most wealthy in Derbyshire with Tong Castle in Shropshire, and a manor house in Staffordshire. They were again appointed to offices of national importance. His son, Sir Richard Vernon VII, was member of Parliament for Derbyshire and Staffordshire, succeeded his father as Treasurer of Calais (1451-2) and became Knight Constable of England. His son Sir Henry, who greatly extended the family's landholdings in Derbyshire and acquired the manor of Bakewell, was appointed Governor and Treasurer of the Household of Prince Arthur and attended his marriage to Catherine of Aragon, later the wife of Arthur's younger brother Henry VIII.

His grandson, Sir George Vernon, was known as 'The King of the Peak' because of his lavish lifestyle and generous hospitality. He proved to be the last male of the Vernon line at Haddon. The Vernons of Sudbury, barons Vernon, descend from his uncles Humphrey and John. On Sir George's death in 1565 the estate passed to his daughter who, legend insists, had eloped with Sir John Manners in 1563. In fact, Sir John was a most eligible suitor, probably welcomed by Sir George.

THE MANNERS

The Manners family were no less influential at Court. Sir John Manners' father was 1st Earl of Rutland, a Knight of the Garter, and a favourite of Henry VIII. He was present at the King's marriage to Ann Boleyn and escorted Anne of Cleves to England as her chamberlain. Sir John's nephew, Roger Manners, 5th Earl of Rutland, was a particularly intriguing character. Imprisoned in the Tower for his association with the Earl of Essex's rebellion in 1600, he was only released because of the close friendship between the Manners family and Sir Robert Cecil. The fine of £30,000 (in 1600!) was later commuted to £10,000. He is also one of the principal claimants to Shakespeare's pen, after Sir Francis Bacon and the Earl of Oxford!

Celebrations at Haddon Hall of the coming of age of the 9th Duke of Rutland 24th September 1907

The life of Sir John's own son was less controversial. Knighted by King James I in 1623, he and his wife Grace founded Lady Manners' School 'for the better instructinge of the male Children of the inhabitants of Bakewell and Great Rowsley'. The school is now a thriving mixed comprehensive under the control of Derbyshire LEA.

Sir George and Lady Grace's son, Sir John, inherited Belvoir Castle and the earldom of Rutland in 1642 on the death of his cousin, the 7th Earl, who had no children. Throughout the Civil War he remained a moderate parliamentarian. When Charles I convened parliament in Oxford in 1643, he was one of 22 peers who absented themselves. Belvoir Castle was besieged by Royalist troops for two years. In 1647 Fairfax ordered that it should become a parliamentary garrison and by 1649 it had suffered severe damage. The Earl was eventually compensated and rebuilding began at Belvoir in 1668. Haddon, however, survived the Civil War intact and remained the principal family home until they moved to Belvoir at the turn of the century.

In the 19th century, the then Lord John Manners, younger son of the 5th Duke of Rutland and himself later the 7th Duke, was a leading member of the 'Young England' group in Parliament around 1840. Numbering Disraeli among its members it advocated a return to the rule of a benevolent aristocracy. Although not fully achieving its aim, it did have some effect on the policy of the government of the time.

Derbyshire DE24 2EB

Tel: 01629 733518

Fax: 01629 732671

reception@thepeacockatrowsley.com

www.thepeacockatrowsley.com

THE PEACOCK AT ROWSLEY

The Peacock at Rowsley is a small luxury hotel located in the famous Peak District in the heart of England, and conveniently close to the major towns of Chesterfield, Sheffield, Manchester, Nottingham and Derby. Recently acquired by Lord Edward Manners, the hotel has been refurbished throughout and styled by award winning designer India Mahdavi.

The 16 comfortable en-suite bedrooms are luxuriously appointed with antique furniture, crisp white sheets and the finest fabrics sourced from London, Paris, New York and Milan. The Peacock is famed for its seven miles of fly fishing on the Rivers Wye and Derwent where anglers come from all over the world to fish for rare wild rainbow trout and the unique strain of brown trout found here. The Peacock is ideally located for visiting nearby Haddon Hall and Chatsworth House.

The Peacock aims to provide a relaxed and comfortable experience, whether for a weekend in the country, a special occasion, or just to eat and drink.

Digital photographs: Adrian Houston